Sweet!

THE DELICIOUS STORY OF CANDY

ANN LOVE & JANE DRAKE

Illustrated by Claudia Dávila

TUNDRA BOOKS

This book is dedicated to the sweet memory of our mother, Kathleen Barnett,
who liked her black balls two at a time.
A.L. and J.D.

To my husband, Michael, who is sweeter than chocolate.
C.D.

Acknowledgments

We extend a chocolate-dipped thank-you to Kathy Lowinger for the opportunity to write this book. Special thanks to Sue Tate for her editorial quality control – as careful and precise as the measurements for a perfect confection. And, purple lollipops of gratitude to all the hardworking staff at Tundra Books.

We would also like to thank Ruth Drake-Alloway; Sam Alloway; Nip Armstrong; Doreen Barnett; Henry Barnett; Ian and Will Barnett; Sadie Barnett; Olga Bondarenko; Trish Brooks; Jennifer Cayley; Lina and Susie Choi of Mother's Sweet and Nut Shop; Jane Morley Cobden; Barb Cochrane; Jane Crist; Dot of Dot's; Geraldine and Paula Draimin; Brian, Jim, Madeline, and Stephanie Drake; Jessie Drake; Ron Dueck; Ganong Bros., Limited; Manju Gheewala; Pat Hancock; Margie Stockwell-Hart; Sally and Tom Hawk; Julie Hunt; Adrian, David, Jennifer, and Melanie Love; Janet and Penny McClure; Wendy Corrigan McCreath; Anne and Murray McDonald; Donna O'Connor; Diane Peck; Daniel Poncelet of Le Chocolat Belge Daniel Ltée; Maria and Steven Price; Dr. James Purves; Dr. W. Timothy Purves; Luke and Olivia Racine; Magy Salmoni; Mark and Mason Salmoni; Colin Shaw; Connie Simoni of Jelly Belly Candy Company; Harold Smith; Birgitta van Swinderen; Mary Thompson; and Howard Wood.

Text copyright © 2007 by Ann Love and Jane Drake
Illustrations copyright © 2007 by Claudia Dávila

Published in Canada by Tundra Books,
75 Sherbourne Street, Toronto, Ontario M5A 2P9

Published in the United States by Tundra Books of Northern New York,
P.O. Box 1030, Plattsburgh, New York 12901

Library of Congress Control Number: 2006903590

Library and Archives Canada Cataloguing in Publication

Love, Ann
Sweet! The delicious story of candy / Ann Love, Jane
Drake ; illustrated by Claudia Dávila.

ISBN 978-0-88776-752-4

    1. Candy – Juvenile literature. 2. Candy – History – Juvenile literature.
    I. Drake, Jane II. Dávila, Claudia III. Title.
TX792.L69 2007   j641.8'53   C2006-902082-5

We acknowledge the financial support of the Government of Canada through the Book Publishing Industry Development Program (BPIDP) and that of the Government of Ontario through the Ontario Media Development Corporation's Ontario Book Initiative.
We further acknowledge the support of the Canada Council for the Arts and the Ontario Arts Council for our publishing program.

ONTARIO ARTS COUNCIL
CONSEIL DES ARTS DE L'ONTARIO

Medium: Digital
Design: Terri Nimmo

Printed and bound in China

1 2 3 4 5 6   12 11 10 09 08 07

CONTENTS

HOW SWEET IT IS!

Sweet Memories

When you choose your favorite candy, do you madly tear off the packaging, or open it slowly, enjoying the familiar rustle of the wrapper?

If it's a bag of jelly beans, do you pick one color carefully, or pop a whole handful into your mouth? Do you hold a marshmallow for a moment between your lips, teasing the taste buds at the tip of your tongue, or do you bite sharply to feel it part softly between your teeth?

With a chunk of chocolate, do you gnaw one end, releasing the sweet scent, or crunch down, chew hard, and swallow fast? Perhaps you start a lollipop by licking

c. 6000 B.C.

SPAIN: on a cave wall, an artist draws a human figure scooping wild honey from a hive high up a tree

slowly, checking to see the color glisten, but finish by crushing the nub off the stick with your teeth. Maybe you like to hold a caramel on your tongue until your mouth fills with syrup, or, with a nougat bar, roll the broken nuts lazily across your tongue and into your cheeks before swallowing. Whatever you do, it's your way and you love it.

And, chances are, the inventors of your favorite candy had fun imagining how you would eat it. Good candy-makers choose ingredients and mixtures for flavor as well as color, smell, texture, and even the sound a candy creates – through licking, slurping, biting, savoring, swallowing, and digesting.

This book tells the stories of inspired candy-makers and the yummy ingredients they used through time and across continents. Trace honey, licorice, marshmallow, sugar, chocolate, and other key sweets from their discovery to today's latest creations. Visit candy-makers working beside campfires, inside temples, at country fairs, in kitchens, and along assembly lines. Find out which candies satisfied the cravings of kids from prehistoric times to the present – from Egyptian boy kings to medieval milkmaids to your great-grandparents to you. And before you turn each page, read the time line for "sweet" facts, including when people realized eating too much candy was linked to tooth decay and poor health.

The story of candy is magical, captivating, and adventurous – just like eating your favorite sweet.

---

c. 4000 B.C.   *c.* 3000 B.C.   *c.* 2600 B.C.

● PAPUA NEW GUINEA: islanders cut sugarcane for its sweet sap

● CHINA: herbalists extract an intensely sweet medicine from licorice root
● IRAQ: Sumerian diners invent toothpicks – the earliest record of dental care

● EGYPT: first-known beekeepers produce honey to embalm the dead, make cosmetics, heal wounds, and offer to the gods

5

Animal Appetites: Sweet Cravings

An August thunderstorm drenches the cows and gives them a few moments' rest from flies. When the sun breaks through, Blossom, the lead female, notices that apples have blown onto the cows' side of the electric fence. Her big lips roll over the stem and leaves of one, then her teeth sink into the flesh. Sweet fills her mouth and she snares another apple. The older cows snatch up apples as fast as they can, juice dribbling out of their mouths.

The calves grab what falls their way, while the bull bulldozes his way through the herd, inhaling greedy mouthfuls until all the fruit within reach is gone.

But the cows aren't satisfied. A calf breaks the wire, allowing the herd into forbidden territory. The animals glom more apples, pears, and tender flowers, then invade the vegetable garden, bulging with late-summer produce. They devour everything. When the farmer comes out from lunch, the herd is flopped in the shade of the apple trees, groaning and passing wind.

Meanwhile, in a parking lot north of Toronto, Jessie, a black Labrador retriever, waits patiently in the car

c. 2000 B.C.

EGYPT: the earliest marshmallows are made by mixing honey with the root sap of the mallow plant that grows in marshes along the Nile

with a snoozing dad while the rest of the family shops. She sniffs out the window, keeping one eye on the store door and one on Dad. Inside the car, the smells are worth investigating. What's this gift-wrapped treat? A few nibbles reveal a sweet pasty substance. In a matter of seconds, two cups of sugar, a pound of red maraschino cherries, vanilla, and more disappear down the dog's throat. Telltale crumbs are all that remain of the mom's special fudge, and soon Jessie knows what it's like to be as sick as a dog.

Cows and dogs aren't the only creatures with cravings. Healthy human bodies often demand sweets. Tons of exercise, playing in the school recital, or a stressful exam may trigger a desire for ice cream or sour gummies. Sometimes activity causes your body to run low on nutrients, making you crave pasta with a sweet cream sauce or a fruit drink to top up your tank. And there are times when your body has been trained to expect sugar. When you spike a fever, celebrate a birthday, or even visit your grandparents, your body awaits a sugar load. And candy can be the ultimate comfort food. If a friend has chicken pox, you can make her a card and a sweet treat in hopes she'll feel better soon. Unlike Blossom and Jessie, most people try to control their cravings, most of the time.

c. 1200 B.C.   *c.* 1000 B.C.

● INDIA: the tradition of serving sweets to guests begins – honey, sweet butter, condensed milk, and pieces of sugarcane
● EGYPT: temple slaves make "honeycakes," the first candies, from dates, seeds, and nuts, all rolled in honey

● GREECE: small fruits, flowers, seeds, and plant stems are candied with honey or with syrup made from figs or dates
● EGYPT: because rodents have strong teeth, some toothache sufferers place live mice on their gums to relieve pain

Sweet Ingestion

Are most kids programmed to love candy? Doctors say yes, even newborn babies enjoy the taste of sugar. Medical science questions if a love for sweets is a survival instinct from prehistoric times – sweet-tasting foods are usually safe to eat while poisonous ones are often bitter. Whatever the reason, we love candy and our brain is the nerve center of its enjoyment.

EYES "Hey, that's good-looking candy!" Your eyes send a message to your brain and you think *yum!*

FINGERS Your fingertips feel the candy's surface and sense its weight; you start predicting what's inside.

NOSE The candy passes under your nose and thousands of specialized nerve receptors inhale its delicious scent.

LIPS Your lips record its texture and temperature.

TEETH *Crunch.* Even if you close your lips, you hear your own chewing, sucking, and swallowing, as the sounds travel up your jawbone into your ears.

TONGUE Molecules of candy mix with your saliva and then penetrate thousands of taste buds inside your mouth. Taste buds that identify sweet are usually clustered on the tip of your tongue; those for sour and salt lie mostly along the sides; and the buds for bitter lie along the back. The more you move

c. 700 B.C.

c. 500 B.C.

ITALY: Etruscans carve dentures from ox teeth, set in gold bands

IRAN: Persians nibble on spices mixed with crystals made from sugarcane

8

a candy around inside your mouth, the more you activate the taste buds for sweet. Candies that are sweet 'n' sour or sweet 'n' salty, like lemon drops or caramel corn, excite a combination of taste buds and give you a full-mouth candy rush. But sweet always registers first.

THROAT Swallowing triggers taste buds in your throat. At the same time, the candy's scent moves up into the back of your nose and reactivates your smell receptors.

STOMACH In your stomach, the "sweet" ride ends. So, you pop another candy into your mouth, and your brain cries *yum* again.

INTESTINES The sugar in candy breaks down to glucose – energy sugar – that is absorbed quickly into your blood. Your brain knows when you've had too much and stores extra glucose in your liver, in case you need it quickly. Excess glucose is stored as fat. *Oops!*

LEGS All that sugar . . . and you feel like running.

c. 400 B.C. *c.* 323 B.C. *c.* 100 B.C.

● IRAQ: villagers dry dates in the sun so they last longer and taste sweeter

● IRAQ: mourners preserve the body of Alexander the Great in honey for the journey to his final resting place in Egypt

● CHINA: cooks sweeten food with maltose, a sugary juice they extract from sweet sorghum grass

Excretions, Oozings, and Saps

Where do sweet flavors come from? Would you believe bee barf, mammal secretions, aphid poop, stem sap, root pulp, and bean fat?
Just look at the natural sources of sweet used by people, past and present.

From Animals

HONEY A worker honeybee sucks nectar from flowers, swallows some for food, and stores the rest in a special stomach where the nectar mixes with saliva. Back at the hive, the bee regurgitates the nectar into the mouth of another worker bee. That bee vomits it again into a cell in the honeycomb, where worker bees fan it vigorously with their wings. As the nectar mixes with saliva and air, it thickens into honey.

MILK Cow's, sheep's, and goat's milk reduce into sweet thick paste or flakes when evaporated slowly.

HONEYDEW Aphids feed on the juices inside stems, leaves, and flowers. At certain times of the year, these insects excrete a sugary liquid called honeydew from their anuses onto tree trunks and leaves. Oddly enough, the Roman scholar Pliny the Elder knew honeydew was a secretion, but guessed it was perspiration from the sky or saliva from the stars – not insect poop.

c. A.D. 50	A.D. 77	*c.* A.D. 100
● ITALY: Romans relieve toothaches with eardrops made from olive oil and boiled earthworms	● ITALY: Pliny the Elder advises his students to eat mint to stimulate their minds	● GREECE: gum lovers chew beeswax mixed with sap from the mastic tree ● ITALY: Romans munch on dates, stuffed with almonds and sometimes candied in honey

From Plants

SUGAR Juice pressed, boiled, crystallized, and refined from the long stems of the sugarcane plant makes up about two-thirds of the world's table sugar. The other third comes from the juice pressed out of sugar beets after the roots are steeped and softened in hot water.

SYRUPS Ancient civilizations evaporated juice from dates, figs, or coconuts to make sweet syrups. Some crushed reeds and grains for juice and boiled it down to a syrupy jelly. Saps from date and sugar palms as well as sugar maple and birch trees are still reduced into syrups. In the last fifty years, food scientists found they could make intensely sweet syrup from ground corn kernels – nearly all sugar-sweetened soft drinks and caramels use corn syrup.

CHOCOLATE After curing and roasting, cocoa beans are compressed until the fatty cocoa butter oozes out and leaves bitter cocoa powder behind. Then some cocoa butter is worked back in, to give chocolate its smooth sheen and velvety, melt-in-your-mouth feel.

Add honey, milk, honeydew, sugar, syrups, or chocolate to crushed leaves (e.g., mint), pressed or grated fruits and peels (e.g., lemon), pulverized flowers (e.g., rose), squished roots (e.g., licorice), globs of tree resin (e.g., chicle), cracked or ground nuts (e.g., almonds), and you get candy. Really!

c. A.D. 250

● INDIA: confectioners shape little figures of animals and people out of sugar

11

Sweet Country

Canadian kids know that biting into maple sugar makes the tip of your tongue swell with flavor.

Americans spend more than $125 million a year on marshmallows. Half the marshmallows sold in summer are toasted over campfires.

Candied pumpkin, tamarind, and squash? Tasty in Mexico!

Brazilians live where both sugarcane and cacao trees grow. Home sweet home!

"Would you like half my candy bar or a millionth of it?"

Many kids around the world enjoy sharing candy with friends. At one time or another, everyone likes to divvy up pieces – fairly or unfairly – hoard chunks, choose the best colors, drool candy juice, show off half-eaten gobs, earn candy rewards, and joke around with their favorite sweets. Interestingly though, kids often prefer candy from their own part of the world and think sweets from other countries taste yucky or look gross.

c. A.D. 300

PERU: the first popcorn popper is a shallow pot with one handle carved in the figure of a cat

ITALY: Roman doctors coat the rims of their patients' cups with honey to help the medicine go down

Scottish kids choose their sweeties – will that be soor plooms, Edinburgh rock, gobstoppers, Jeddart snails, or curly-murlies?

Dutch kids chomp the heads off their extra-salty licorice animals, then eat the legs and bodies.

Baguette and chocolate-bar sandwiches – only in France?

In Greece and Turkey, kids eat honey-drenched pastry called baklava like candy – with lots of finger licking.

In Armenia, kids love strawberry *bastegh*, a stiff fruit paste hung out to dry on a sunny day.

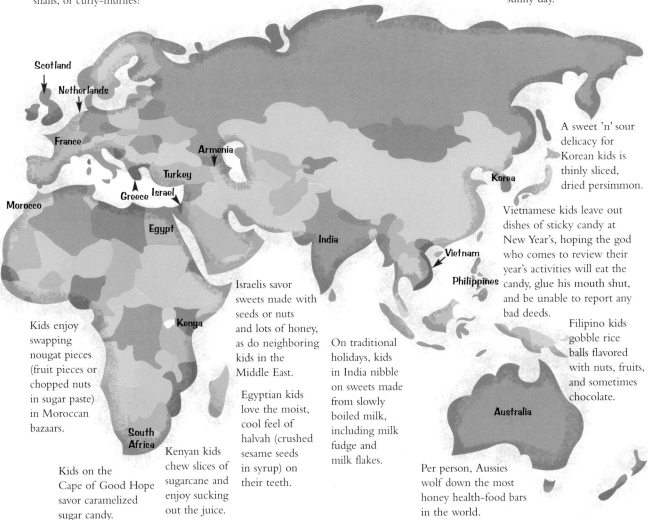

Scotland

Netherlands

France

Morocco

Armenia

Turkey

Greece   Israel

Egypt

Korea

India

Vietnam

Philippines

Kenya

Australia

South Africa

A sweet 'n' sour delicacy for Korean kids is thinly sliced, dried persimmon.

Vietnamese kids leave out dishes of sticky candy at New Year's, hoping the god who comes to review their year's activities will eat the candy, glue his mouth shut, and be unable to report any bad deeds.

Filipino kids gobble rice balls flavored with nuts, fruits, and sometimes chocolate.

Kids enjoy swapping nougat pieces (fruit pieces or chopped nuts in sugar paste) in Moroccan bazaars.

Israelis savor sweets made with seeds or nuts and lots of honey, as do neighboring kids in the Middle East.

Egyptian kids love the moist, cool feel of halvah (crushed sesame seeds in syrup) on their teeth.

On traditional holidays, kids in India nibble on sweets made from slowly boiled milk, including milk fudge and milk flakes.

Per person, Aussies wolf down the most honey health-food bars in the world.

Kids on the Cape of Good Hope savor caramelized sugar candy.

Kenyan kids chew slices of sugarcane and enjoy sucking out the juice.

c. A.D. 400

c. A.D. 450

● ITALY: wealthy Romans gorge on honeyed almonds

● CENTRAL AMERICA: Mayans chew chicle from the sapodilla tree to help digest food and quench thirst
● IRAN: Persians boil sugarcane with limewater and bullock's blood to make hard cone-shaped loaves of white sugar crystals

13

PRIMAL SWEETS

Honey, Honey

When you bite into a sesame snap, the honey that spreads sweetly across your tongue is the same liquid gold that kids licked off their lips and fingertips thousands of years ago. It is made by the same kind of bee, but with different methods of beekeeping.

Prehistoric Honey

Honeybees originated in Asia and spread through Europe and Africa in prehistoric times. People found wild beehives by luck or by beelining – following bees as they flew away from a flower patch.

Collecting honey from wild hives is dangerous because bees prefer to nest high in trees. Prehistoric gatherers had to scramble up trunks, cling to branches, swat stinging bees, and, at the same time, grab chunks of honeycomb. At some point, people discovered that bees can be calmed with smoke and started arming themselves with smudge pots. When most raids ended, the bees and hive were destroyed.

How did prehistoric kids eat honey? No one knows for sure, but they likely poked sticks or fingers into honeycomb and sucked them clean.

Beekeeping: c. 2600 B.C. to c. A.D. 1850

Ancient Egyptians observed that, every now and then, half the bees in a hive

c. A.D. 500

● CENTRAL AMERICA: Mayans sip a chocolate drink made from cocoa powder for energy
● MIDDLE EAST: herdsmen crunch on honey and sesame-seed brittle
● SPAIN: the taste for licorice is so popular, farmers grow the plant as a crop as well as gathering wild roots

● CHINA: tart loquat, pear, and plum syrups are made from unripe fruit
● SIBERIA: neither sugarcane nor honeybees reach the Far North, but kids can enjoy birch sap in spring, flower nectar and wild berries in summer

would separate into a swarm and fly off to start another hive. As the swarm formed, the bees were quiet and could be coaxed to settle in a specially prepared hollow log or mud cylinder. In ancient Greece, beekeepers found they got fewer stings if they harvested honey from back doors cut into the hives. In northern Europe, people used upside-down straw baskets, or skeps, for hives. Bees crammed skeps with honeycomb and their keepers harvested the honey after dunking the hive in water and drowning the bees. Skeps traveled with European settlers on clipper ships around the world. Bees found new flowers and their honey took on slightly different flavors, but still tasted like honey.

In ancient times, kids enjoyed sweetmeats – honeyed vegetables, fruits, nuts, or grains. The first "candy" was made from honey cooked with nuts, seeds, and scented waters. If the honey boiled a long time, it hardened into brittle. Less time boiling and the honey cooled into chewy jelly similar to Turkish delight. From medieval times onward, kids were suckers for suckets – small fruits or fruit slices spiced and candied in honey. And you can bet kids finished their sweets by licking the honey off their lips and fingertips.

Honey Supernatural

People once believed that bees didn't make honey, but collected it from a secret source. Honey was a wondrous mystery and the food of gods.

We now know that honey is made from flower nectar and bee saliva, dehydrated by worker bees fanning the mixture with their wings. In her short lifetime, a worker bee may travel 800 kilometers (497 miles) foraging for nectar, but, after all that, produce less than a teaspoonful of honey. And, believe it or not, worker bees share information about the direction and distance to a good nectar patch through the steps of a dance they perform inside the hive.

Four discoveries in the nineteenth century made it possible for beekeepers to help their bees make honey.

In 1851, Reverend Langstroth of Pennsylvania found that if boxlike hives were fitted with removable, internal frames and if the distance between the frames was the width of two bees, the bees would build their honeycomb on the frames and not jam the space in between with their cells. And if the distance above and below the frames was the width of just one bee, the bees would not build there either. So, with proper "bee spaces," the frames could be removed for harvesting honey without killing the bees or wrecking their hives.

In 1857, Johannes Mehring from Germany found if he placed sheets of beeswax prestamped with hexagonal cell outlines inside the frames, the bees would build their cells on the sheets in an orderly way, making safe honey removal even easier.

In 1865, Abbé Collin of France invented a mesh sheet to cover the first story of a stacking hive to keep the large queen in the bottom level. Smaller worker bees could crawl through the mesh to store honey in frames above the "queen excluder." Then the beekeeper could remove the upper frames without

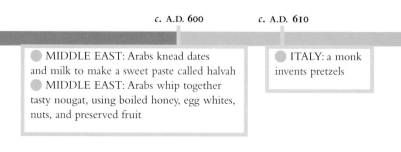

c. A.D. 600

MIDDLE EAST: Arabs knead dates and milk to make a sweet paste called halvah

MIDDLE EAST: Arabs whip together tasty nougat, using boiled honey, egg whites, nuts, and preserved fruit

c. A.D. 610

ITALY: a monk invents pretzels

disturbing the queen's nursery and their honey supply, isolated in the bottom story.

In 1865, Francesco de Aruschka of Austria invented a honey extractor, using centrifugal force to pull honey from the comb once the caps have been cut off the cells.

Next time you polish off a fruit-and-honey bar, sesame snap, or granola bar, consider how far the bees had to fly in order to sweeten your taste buds. How many bees joined the dance to find the nectar? How many wing beats did it take to reduce the nectar to honey?

Even though we know a lot more about honey and bees today, honey is still a supernatural substance.

17

Sweet Milk

Go to the refrigerator and pour yourself a glass of milk. Sniff it and decide if it's sweet or savory. Or does it just smell like milk – the stuff you're supposed to drink for strong bones and good health? When it's boiled down and the 87% that is water evaporates, milk becomes sweet syrup, used for centuries as a base for candy or desserts. And milk has also been churned and frozen into one of the world's favorite sweets – ice cream.

In India, *halvais* turn *rabadi* into *mithai*. Mithai are sweets made by confectioners called halvais who use reduced milk, or rabadi, as their main ingredient. As Indian as curry, mithai are prepared for all imaginable occasions, from kite-flying festivals to weddings to Hindu New Year to celebrating a new home. There's even a candy for saying good-bye – to sweeten a parting. When a boy is born, the family receives nutritious and valuable *penda* – mithai made

from whole milk and sugar. And kids love *rusgula* – a pink or white coconut-flavored candy made with curdled milk that's dipped in sugar syrup. All are popular ways to savor a milky sweet.

Cold milk also has sweet possibilities. . . . The keepers of ice-cream history say the first scoop was made possible over three thousand years ago, when the Chinese started putting winter ice into special icehouses for use year-round. Marco Polo, the Venetian world traveler, is credited with bringing the knowledge of iced sweets home to Italy from China in the

c. A.D. 700

● EUROPE: tooth cavities are filled with stone chips or pine resin – sometimes even stale bread, candle wax, or raven dung

c. A.D. 710

● EGYPT: Arabs plant sugarcane

c. A.D. 720

● IRAQ: Arabs open a distillery in Baghdad to make rose water

fourteenth century. If so, why did it take until 1565 for the first Italian gelato to be made? And how could Emperor Akbar of India have enjoyed ice cream with saffron and pistachio nuts in 1556 when he lived where it rarely freezes? Up until 1649, Charles I of England supposedly kept the recipe for ice cream secret. After he was beheaded, nobles may have suffered ice-cream headaches as they gorged on this newly available delicacy. But before electricity was discovered, ice was hard to find. Has the evidence run cold, or has it melted like ice cream itself?

Ice cream has a murky past, with secret recipes and closely guarded techniques. When the hand-cranked freezer was invented in 1846, ice cream was soon available to more than a few elite. But it was the invention of the continuous freezer in 1926 that brought ice cream into the mainstream. Ever since then, "I scream, you scream, we all scream for ice cream."

c. A.D. 750

CHINA: licorice root, ginger, and ground nuts are filled with sugar for a tasty treat

c. A.D. 754

JAPAN: Jian Zhen, a Buddhist monk, masks the flavor of his medicines with sugar

Fruity to Gummy

Hack! Hack! Achoo! What do you reach for when you have a runny nose and sore throat? A Gummi Worm? Not likely. But, strange as it seems, the idea of gummy candy probably came from old cold medicines.

First, the fruit flavor. Kids have enjoyed the summer-sweet taste of fruit for thousands of years. In the ancient Middle East, they ate dried dates and figs for candy. Romans replaced the stones of dried dates with almonds to munch on at feasts. Ancient Chinese nibbled dried peaches, jujubes (a kind of date), and mei plums (a kind of apricot) for a sweet pick-me-up. On the Great Plains of North America, aboriginal peoples mashed ripe berries, rolled the paste flat, and dried it in the sun to make chewy, sweet fruit leather.

Then someone thought to add gumminess to fruit syrups and make a pleasing finger food. In the Middle Ages, Arabs invented the lozenge, probably using gum from the acacia or mastic tree to harden fruit syrup. Around 1600, Giovanni Pastilla, the Italian confectioner to the queen of France, invented the fruit pastille, probably thickening fruit syrup by boiling. After Pastilla, European pharmacists hardened pastilles with gelatin made from animal skins, ligaments, and bones. They filled pastilles with cold medicines and

c. A.D. 800

MIDDLE EAST: after meals, Arabs rinse with mouthwash and polish their teeth with a small stick and tooth powder
IRAQ: Arab merchant sailors in the Persian Gulf trade sugar, candied capers, rose water, and fruit syrups
FRANCE: King Charlemagne collects honey and beeswax as a tax from farmers

molded them into
small mounds or
squares to dissolve on
the tongue.

In 1922, German candy-maker Hans Riegel cut
the medicine from a gelatin pastille mixture, added lots
of sugar, and molded his
gummy candy into little bears.
Then, in the 1980s, the Trolli
Candy Company in America broke
the cute mold and made Gummi Worms, spiders,
snakes, bugs, bare feet, and roadkill – fun for kids,
disgusting for adults.

The first gummy candies kept sticking together. Pharmacists traditionally
dusted their pastilles with sugar to separate them. Gummi makers
solved the problem in an older way. They
coated their candies with a skin of beeswax to
make it both shiny and less sticky, while still
feeling a little wet and gross.

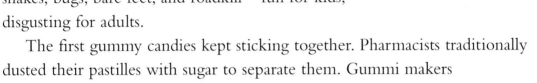

Inventive candy-makers, including Hans Riegel,
never sneeze at dusting off old recipes or changing them a
little to come up with new sensations. *Achoo! Ahem!*

c. A.D. 850

CHINA: diners nibble sugared or
honeyed jujubes
MIDDLE EAST: the most expensive
rose water is made from rose petals
collected by maidens at dawn

21

Maple Sugar Time

The sleigh, with a large metal tank tied on top, heaves forward. Eli clucks at the horses and checks the sky. "The weather's perfect. We'll get the first boil today," he says. "The clearest, sweetest maple syrup there is."

Eighty years of drilling for sap has left the trunks of the sugar maple trees pocked with scars. Eli's father tapped nearly 3,000 trees, but now there's only enough family on the farm to tap 700. And sugaring off the old-fashioned Mennonite way is hard work.

Eli stops the horses at each tree and empties every bucket of sap into the tank. The sap's as see-through as water, but tasting one drop reveals a hint of woody sweetness. Smoke and soft steam drift up from the sugar shack as Eli ties up the horses and siphons the sap from the tank into an outdoor reservoir.

"Gravity will deliver sap as it's needed," Eli explains. "When I open the tap, it'll flow down into the evaporating pan."

Inside, the sugar shack is fitted with deluxe equipment and is spotlessly clean. A stainless steel pan sits on top of a firebox the size of a large dining table. The sap snakes its way through a zigzag ladder of troughs in the pan, changing from a clear fluid at the intake to a rich amber color at the outlet. Eli opens the furnace door and stokes the blaze with trimmings from his brother's sawmill. Jacob, Eli's son, skims froth and tiny particles off the surface of the boiling sap. He looks closely at the color and thickness of the sap closest to the outlet. Then he signals that some of the syrup is ready for its final boil. Together they decant it into a smaller pan on top of a separate mini evaporator.

Eli stays close, watching and waiting for the critical moment. "This won't take long," he explains. "It's easy to overcook. Sap can crystallize, burn, or catch

c. A.D. 900

MIDDLE EAST: Arabs sprinkle nuts, fruits, spices, and sugar on their cakes
NORTH AMERICA: aboriginal kids suck "sapsicles" that form at the ends of sugar maple twigs on cold late-winter mornings
CENTRAL AMERICA: Mayans tend hives of stingless bees whose honey is used in ceremonies

fire in seconds." Suddenly, the rolling boil changes to tiny, air-filled bubbles and the sap rises up in the pan.

"Now for a real treat," Eli says, winking as Jacob disappears outside. He inserts a candy thermometer and waits until the temperature shoots up over 110°C (230°F). Jacob reappears with a tray of clean, packed snow just as the temperature reaches 112°C (234°F). Eli scoops out a ladle of super-hot syrup and dribbles a narrow strip onto the snow. Jacob rolls the hardening syrup onto a stick. With a flick of his wrist, he holds up a glasslike maple lollipop. Is your mouth watering?

c. A.D. 950

c. A.D. 966

● MIDDLE EAST: Arabs invent caramel, but it is used as a hair remover

● ITALY: Venetian traders construct a warehouse to store sugar for trade as medicine in central Europe

Nuts!

When offered a cup of hot chocolate, do you add a marshmallow? Does your tummy growl for maple syrup on your pancakes, butter on your corn, or cream on your strawberries? Some foods just go together and, in the candy world, that includes sugar and nuts.

Almonds

Almonds grow wild in the Middle East and kids there have been shelling them for ten thousand years. The Persians and the Arabs have a long history of candying their almonds. The Arabs invented marzipan, a tempting paste of ground almonds with sugar. They also invented nougat. Stories tell of a Turkish emperor in the mid-eighteenth century who was so addicted to the combination of almonds and sugar that he employed six chefs at Topkapi Palace, each with one hundred apprentices, to make his best-loved sweets.

Today, candied almonds remain a favorite in the Middle East. At modern Iranian weddings, the bride and groom place sugared almonds on each other's tongues. In Afghanistan, kids eat sugared almonds at New Year's so their mouths and lives will stay sweet all year.

Pralines (Prawlins')

The mouthwatering, crispy combination of nuts and caramel was supposedly discovered by kids. In the early seventeenth century, Lassagne was chef of the

c. A.D. 1000

MIDDLE EAST: Arabs invent lozenges
CHINA: the first toothbrushes are made with hog bristles
CRETE: Arabs install the first industrial sugar refinery on the island they call Candia
MIDDLE EAST: Arabs enjoy marzipan

household for the Duke of Plessis-Praslin in France. One day, Lassagne's children stole some almonds from the kitchen and tried cooking them in sugar. The wonderful smell attracted their father, who offered to keep their theft secret if they gave him some. Lassagne perfected the recipe, named the sweet after the duke, and presented the candy to the court of the king. It was a sensation! Lassagne set up a shop to sell his sweets, where pralines are still sold today.

The French carried the recipe to Louisiana, where pecans replaced almonds. In the old French Quarter of New Orleans, street vendors sell prawlins' on warm evenings.

Peanuts

Americans are the inventors of so many lip-smacking ways to eat peanuts. The first peanut brittles probably came from southern kitchens before the Civil War.

Cracker Jack, that tantalizing mixture of caramel-coated popcorn and peanuts, was invented by F.W. Rueckheim of Chicago in 1896. The boy on the box was his grandson, who died at the age of nine.

American candy-makers have invented hundreds of different bars made with peanuts. They have tried more peanuts, fewer peanuts; more chocolate, less chocolate; more caramel, less caramel; some marshmallow, no marshmallow – all searching for the most irresistible sugar and nut combination.

c. A.D. 1050

EUROPE: marsh mallow root sap is thought to cure the common cold

Gum Daddies

Would you buy White Mountain paraffin wax gum or State of Maine Pure Spruce Gum? In the mid-1800s, kids could buy chewing gum, but there were no best-selling brands. And then along came . . .

Santa Anna and Thomas Adams

General Santa Anna won the Battle of the Alamo in 1836, was five-time president of Mexico, and once honored his amputated leg with a state funeral. During the Mexican Revolution, he fled to the United States, taking with him a ton of chicle, resin of the sapodilla tree. He hoped to develop it as a rubber substitute and make his fortune.

Thomas Adams, a New York photographer, joined the general as a business partner. When Santa Anna returned to Mexico, Adams carried on trying to make chicle into tires, boots, toys, masks – nothing worked. In 1871, he was about to throw the whole gooey pile away when he saw a girl order White Mountain gum in a drugstore. Adams remembered chicle was chewed by Mexicans and asked the druggist if he would consider selling a new brand. The druggist agreed and, that night, Adams made a box of Adams New York No. 1 unflavored gum hunks. Adams' "stretching

c. A.D. 1100

● EGYPT: Arabs decorate their feast tables with giant sugar-paste models of trees, buildings, and animals
● EUROPE: candied fruits are popular, but honey is the usual sweetener
● NORTH AMERICA: aboriginal peoples chew spruce-tree resin to relieve toothache and freshen breath

and snapping" gum was an instant success. By 1888, he was making his fortune selling gum balls in vending machines and Black Jack licorice gum in sticks.

William Wrigley, Jr.

As a young man, William Wrigley, Jr. sold soap, then baking powder, in the Chicago area. He gave away chewing gum as a gift with every purchase. When he noticed his gum was more popular than the baking powder, he switched products.

In the early 1900s, Wrigley was the first to advertise gum on billboards and in magazines. His motto was TELL 'EM QUICK AND TELL 'EM OFTEN. When the telephone became popular, he sent a free pack of gum to every subscriber. By 1910, his advertising was paying off – Wrigley's Spearmint was the top-selling gum in the United States.

Frank Fleer and Walter Diemer

Frank Fleer, maker of Chiclets in Philadelphia, wanted to market a fun gum for kids. In 1906, he invented Blibber-Blubber, but it was too sticky and never made it to store shelves. In 1928, Walter Diemer, an accountant for the Frank H. Fleer Gum Company, started experimenting in the lab during breaks. By accident, he discovered bubble gum. The only color available in the lab at the time was pink and his Dubble Bubble has remained pink to this day.

c. A.D. 1150

● EUROPE: Crusaders return with sugar, but only the wealthy can afford it
● ITALY: Venetian traders introduce comfits – tiny sweets made from single seeds, or nuts, or pieces of fruit, covered in layers of colored sugar

SUGAR CANDY

Sugar Plantation

Sugarcane is a giant grass with its stem packed full of sweet-tasting juice. Ancient traders carried wild plants from Papua New Guinea and traded them throughout Southeast Asia.

Eventually in India, cooks discovered if they boiled the juice and dried the syrup in the sun, they got crystals, or *khanda*. Kinda sounds like candy. . . .

King Darius of Persia invaded India about 500 B.C. and returned with what his people called a reed that gives honey without the help of bees. The Persians learned to grow it and make sweets, but kept sugar a secret – as best they could – for centuries. When the Arabs conquered Persia, over a thousand years later, they discovered the possibilities of sugar and planted it across North Africa, southern Spain, and Sicily. Over six hundred years later, Crusaders returned to Western Europe from the Middle East with pieces of sugarcane, starting the biggest sugar craze in history.

Sugarcane needs tropical heat, rich soil, lots of sun and rain, and a steady

c. A.D. 1200

- EUROPE: people believe that unicorns crave licorice
- FRANCE: sugared almonds, or *dragées*, are made for medicinal purposes

breeze. Only the small, southern islands in Europe have that climate, so European explorers took sugarcane on their travels. Plantations soon followed – first on the islands off West Africa, then in the Caribbean and the East Indies. But farming, harvesting, and processing sugarcane without machines was back-breaking work. The plantation owners turned to slaves and, for hundreds of years, the world's sweet tooth was satisfied through the sufferings of slave labor.

Today, plantation owners hire waged workers to operate machines, but the steps from cane to crystal have changed little. When sugarcane is fully grown, workers set it on fire to burn off the leaves. Then giant bulldozers lift the stems into haulers that transport huge quantities to the cleaning plant. There the cane is washed and sliced, then fed through mills, where the stems are smashed, shredded, and pressed. Fiber is separated from the juice, dried, and recycled as fuel for the mills. The juice moves on to the boiler house, where it evaporates in heated pans. Workers add some sugar to the concentrated juice to start it crystallizing and to separate out the molasses. The molasses is trucked off for use in animal feed while the raw sugar crystals are further cleaned, refined, and whitened by heating with lime, filtering through charcoal, and drying with hot air.

Twenty million hectares (77,220 sq. mi.) of sugarcane are cultivated in 121 tropical countries each year. And millions of tons are crafted into candy.

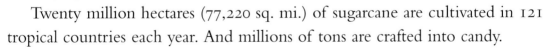

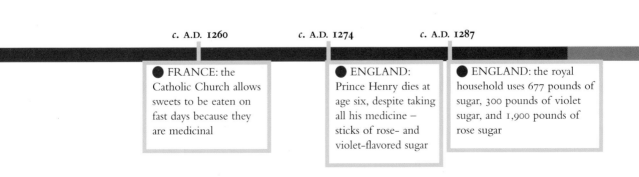

c. A.D. 1260

● FRANCE: the Catholic Church allows sweets to be eaten on fast days because they are medicinal

c. A.D. 1274

● ENGLAND: Prince Henry dies at age six, despite taking all his medicine – sticks of rose- and violet-flavored sugar

c. A.D. 1287

● ENGLAND: the royal household uses 677 pounds of sugar, 300 pounds of violet sugar, and 1,900 pounds of rose sugar

Sweet Chemistry

How many times have you been told that sugar is bad for you? In fact, sugar is an essential food for all plants and animals. Almost everything nutritious you eat – including liver and broccoli – contains natural sugar. The problem is that sugar alone has only calories – no proteins, no fibers, no vitamins, no essential fatty acids, and hardly any minerals. So a diet of pure sugar – even natural sugar – can make you feel full, but is empty of nutrients.

Glucose, sometimes called dextrose, is the basic sugar found in fruits, vegetables, and the blood of animals, including you. Fructose is a simple sugar found in plants, fruits, and honey. Sucrose, found in sugarcane, sugar beets, and maple sap, is a double sugar made up of both glucose and fructose. Sucrose is our regular white table sugar. Other sugars important in nature include lactose in milk and maltose in grains.

Candy, as we love it, is a direct result of what sugar crystals – especially sucrose crystals – do when heated and cooled. First of all, sucrose dissolves completely in water to make syrup. When heated, some of the water evaporates, concentrating the syrup. If a hot sucrose solution is cooled slowly, granules or crystals form. But if the mixture is cooled quickly, the fructose and glucose work against each other, preventing the solution from crystallizing, and a smooth candy forms. If the syrup is thin before it cools, the candy will be chewy, but if the syrup is thick and then cooled, the candy will be hard like glass. Adding ingredients such as milk or lemon juice also affects the chemistry, changing the feel and look of the candy.

When candy-makers started to use sucrose, they found they could play with the textures and appearances of candies more than they could with honey. Then, with the invention of electric stoves and thermometers, they discovered

c. A.D. 1300	A.D. 1319	A.D. 1344
● EUROPE: fashionable kitchens serve thin, crisp white wafers made by pressing sugar and rosewater paste between hot iron tongs ● EUROPE: doctors prescribe *manus Christi*, a medicinal hard candy made from sugar, flowers, rose water, and sometimes gold leaf or pearls	● ENGLAND: Venetian traders sell 50 tons of sugar for £10,800,000 in today's money ($20,460,000 U.S.)	● FRANCE: candied oranges, lemons, limes, and tamarinds are served at the coronation feast for Pope Clement VI

the exact temperatures required to create new and exciting candy effects. Today, when you go to a candy counter, there are so many delightful choices thanks to sugar chemistry – but remember to save room for food that also contains proteins, vitamins, minerals, and other important nutrients. There is sugar in liver and broccoli too!

Candy	Sugar Temperature
peanut brittle, pralines	160°C/320°F
barley sugar, citric acid drops	149°C/300°F
butterscotch candies, humbugs	132°C/270°F
hard caramels, marshmallows	121°C/250°F
soft caramels, chewy toffees	118°C/244°F
fudge, fondant	112°C/234°F

c. A.D. 1390

CHINA: hollow sugar figures become a confectioner's specialty

Medieval Subtleties

If you found yourself at a banquet in medieval Europe, you'd be in for a few surprises. First of all, "banquets" could be day-long feasts, serving only dessert and candy. You wouldn't need to worry about the polite way to hold your fork because you likely wouldn't have one. Good manners were more about not farting, not picking your nose, and not scratching your fleabites at the table. Cleaning up afterwards was easy – cooks pitched pails of slop and kitchen waste right out the window onto the street.

Along with rollicking good times, you'd be entertained by "subtleties" – spectacular table decorations, often created out of the new luxury "spice," sugar. Cooks had discovered how to mix and heat sugar with other ingredients to make dough that could be fashioned into edible shapes. They formed marzipan – made from sugar and ground almonds – into

c. A.D. 1429

● PORTUGAL: Prince Henry succeeds in growing sugarcane on the Canary Islands and Madeira

c. A.D. 1450

● MEXICO: Aztecs believe chocolate has magic powers and use it in religious ceremonies
● TURKEY: Anatolians savor a jelly called *lokum*, made with grape molasses, honey, and flour, later called Turkish delight

A.D. 1452

● ITALY: Pope Nicholas V permits slave labor of "infidels" on sugarcane plantations

snakes, snails, frogs, rabbits, pigeons, and more. They molded sugar paste – made from sugar syrup and tree gum – into objects such as miniature cups, castles, tables, and shields. At the end of the banquet, subtleties were smashed apart and eaten by the guests, or thrown to beggars outside.

At one wedding banquet in Rome in the fifteenth century, the legend of Hercules was created in subtleties. Life-sized sugar-paste sculptures showed the hero fighting a lion, a boar, and a wild bull. At the end of the banquet, the figures were thrown down a staircase and the guests took hunks home.

At the marriage banquet for the Duke of Burgundy and an English princess in 1468, scenes from the duke's orchards were presented in thirty subtleties. Each showcased a different fruit tree, surrounded by dancing harvesters. Little baskets carried by the figures were filled with tiny candied fruits and nuts for the guests to nibble on.

In Italy, confectioners specialized in subtleties made with spun sugar. They heated liquid sugar to very high temperatures and then pulled the hardening syrup into long threads. While still warm, bundles of threads were worked into shapes. At a banquet for King Henry III of France in Venice, everything on the tables was made out of spun sugar – plates, cutlery, goblets, centerpieces, even the tablecloth – 1,286 works of edible art.

Subtleties are out of fashion now, but we enjoy memories of them in wedding cakes and gingerbread houses. Spun sugar has moved from the palace to the fairground, where it lives on in its modern form – candy floss!

A.D. 1487

● ITALY: the Duke of Ferrara serves 118 kg (260 lb.) of sugared almonds, called confetti, at a wedding banquet for his son

33

Sugary Snippets:
A Series of Fortunate Events

How do candy-makers find new ways to turn sugar into popular sweets? By sudden inspiration or happy mistake – if you believe their stories.

Candy Canes

In 1670, the choirmaster of Cologne Cathedral in Germany gave out sticks of sugar candy to keep his young singers quiet during sermons. When he picked up sugar sticks for the Christmas service, they were still warm and bendable. In a moment of fun and in the spirit of the season, the choirmaster got the idea to curve the ends of the sticks to look like shepherds' crooks.

Rock Candy

In the early 1800s in Edinburgh, Scotland, Alexander Ferguson – a.k.a. Sweetie Sandy – left a batch of hard candy, unwrapped, in his warm factory for several days. When he found it again, the centers had crystallized. He liked the way the candy turned soft in his mouth, and so did his customers.

Saltwater Taffy

In 1883 in Atlantic City, New Jersey, David Bradley's taffy shop was flooded with seawater during a storm. Because he'd worked hard – pulling the cooling candy by hand to make it smooth and glossy – David wasn't prepared to throw out his damaged stock. So he rinsed it off and sold it as saltwater taffy. His taffy became a fad – not

A.D. 1506

● DOMINICAN REPUBLIC: Pedro d'Arranca successfully grows sugarcane. A sweet harvest with a sour history – slavery takes root in the Americas

because it was made with seawater, but because it was a great souvenir from a seaside town.

Fudge

In the late 1880s, in a New England women's college dormitory, a group of students apparently set out to make caramel. They botched the recipe, but found they liked eating their mistake. They called their candy "fudge," a popular slang word at the time meaning "foolishness."

Lollipops

The ancient Egyptians, Chinese, and Arabs ate gooey sweets off sticks. Late eighteenth- and early nineteenth-century street vendors in London sold hard candies known as "lollipops," but not necessarily on sticks.

Our modern, mass-produced lollipop is an American invention. One story claims that in 1905, workers at the McAviney Candy Company of America stirred the vats of cooking candy with sticks. At day's end, the owner took home the used sticks, with candy hardening on the tips, as treats for his kids. Seeing how much they loved their treats, he started to mass-produce them. But McAviney did not give lollipops their name. George Smith, another American candy-maker, trademarked "Lolly Pop," which he said was the name of his favorite racehorse.

These candies may have been invented by inspiration or luck – but they succeeded because sugar can take on so many exciting flavors, shapes, and textures.

A.D. 1526

● INDIA: between battles, Mogul leaders nibble on sweetmeats made from sugar, almonds, and coconut

A.D. 1533

● FRANCE: Catherine de Médicis brings her secret Italian recipe for gelato to France when she marries the king

A.D. 1535

● ENGLAND: the mayor of Coventry welcomes visiting dukes with a banquet of dessert and candies called comfits, leaches, marchpane, jumbles, and suckets

A.D. 1545

● FRANCE: the famous Parisian surgeon, Ambroise Paré, specializes in filling decayed teeth with cork and lead

Jelly Beans

Candy factories don't encourage visitors. If you take a tour, you may get to view some of the assembly line – but only through windows. Why? Because candy-makers must keep their workplace spotlessly clean. And they don't want anyone getting a good look at their ingredients, recipes, machines, or processes.

So, let's take a forbidden peek into a jelly-bean factory. Wash your hands; put on a sterile, factory-issue hairnet, coat, gloves, and boots. Keep your pencil, notepad, and camera out of sight.

First impressions? Giant vats, drums, buckets, bins, pans, scoops, trays, kettles, conveyer belts, hoppers . . . the cheerful noise of machines sorting, stirring, and mixing . . . and the overwhelmingly sweet smell of warm sugar.

In this factory, jelly-bean production starts in shiny copper kettles, where the ingredients for the soft centers – sugar and corn syrup – are stirred and heated. Jelly-bean centers aren't usually flavored or colored, but are just sweet and chewy.

Meanwhile, a nearby machine fills tray after tray with powdery cornstarch. The trays move along a conveyer belt to a casting machine that presses curved jelly-bean shapes into the cornstarch, forming little molds for the centers. Next, the trays pass under nozzles that squirt the sugar and corn syrup mixture, piped hot from the kettles, into the molds. Then the trays are stacked while the centers set.

Next morning, a machine tips the trays to separate the centers from the cornstarch. The cornstarch is recycled back to the beginning of the assembly line to make new molds. The centers pass through a steam bath, are sprayed with sugar, and left to dry on trays.

c. A.D. 1550

PORTUGAL: candied fruit-jelly pastes are cut into portions called marmelada
NORTHERN EUROPE: when monasteries close during the Protestant Reformation, honey production drops

On day three, the sugar-coated jelly-bean centers are tossed into heated drums that look and rotate like little cement mixers. Workers add scoops of granulated sugar along with pots of liquid color and flavor, one color per drum. As they tumble in the drums, a colored, sugar shell forms on each jelly-bean center. The shell thickens as more and more sugar is added.

The jelly beans cool on trays before returning to the drums for polishing. Beeswax or carnauba wax is added to glaze the jelly beans while they tumble to a bright shine. Finally, different colors of jelly beans are mixed together and packaged for sale.

Hand back your hairnet, gloves, coat, and boots . . . and collect your free pack of jelly beans. Next time you toss a handful of jelly beans into your mouth, will you remember that they took three days to make? Or will you just enjoy them?

A.D. 1578   A.D. 1580   c. A.D. 1590

MOROCCO: Ahmed el Mansour starts building el Badii Palace and pays for his construction materials with their weight in sugar

SPAIN: the first cocoa processing plant is established

FRANCE: Benedictine nuns make barley-sugar triangles with a secret ingredient – "perlimpinpin"

The Scoop on Ice-Cream Cones

What's the difference between dessert and candy? If candy is sweet finger food, eaten away from the table and between meals, then ice cream in a dish is dessert, but ice cream in an edible cone is candy.

At the opening of the St. Louis World's Fair in 1904 (celebrating the Louisiana Purchase), over fifty stands sold ice cream either in paper cups, off reusable glass sticks called penny licks, or in paper wrappings as "hokey pokey." Meanwhile, a dozen concessions sold hot sugary waffles. But when the fair was over, the ice-cream and waffle vendors had teamed up and their happy customers were licking scoops of ice cream in sugar-crusted waffle cones.

WAFFLES
come and get 'em!

you'll all scream for
ICE CREAM

c. A.D. 1600   A.D. 1602

● ENGLAND: a German diplomat describes the black, sugar-rotted teeth of Queen Elizabeth I and her courtiers

● ENGLAND: a book on gentlewomanly pastimes instructs how to make candied rose petals – right on the rosebush

Which of these vendors at the fair deserves credit for turning ice cream into candy? They all claimed to have been the one who invented the ice-cream cone.

Ernest Hamwi, a Syrian American, operated a concession at the St. Louis World's Fair, where he sold a wafer-thin treat called *zalabia*, a traditional pastry from the Middle East. Hamwi said that, when the ice-cream stand next to him ran out of dishes, he formed his hot zalabias around a cone-shaped tool he had on hand, and offered the edible cones as ice-cream containers.

Italo Marciony, an Italian American, got tired of people breaking or walking away with his penny-lick sticks. So he invented a waffle cup and took out a patent for it a year before the fair. He arrived at the St. Louis World's Fair each night with a supply of his waffle cups – but afterwards, when cones became popular, the courts said his cups weren't cones and wouldn't give him exclusive rights to manufacture them.

Charles and Frank Menches, American brothers who claimed to have invented the hamburger, ran ice-cream concessions throughout the Midwest. One woman bought ice cream at their stand at the St. Louis World's Fair while she was eating a waffle. She peeled a layer off the waffle to hold her ice cream when it started to drip. The brothers said they grabbed her idea and made cones by forming hot waffles around a tool they used to put up their tent.

Some say the ice-cream cone was invented long before, in Paris or London in a high-class dining room. But those cones were decorations on a dessert plate and the ice cream was eaten with a spoon.

A.D. 1621 *c.* A.D. 1622

c. A.D. 1640

● UNITED STATES: aboriginal peoples introduce a popped corn snack to New England settlers – three hundred years before the first movies

● UNITED STATES: honeybees from England are introduced to Virginia and spread west faster than the settlers

● FRANCE: confectioners discover if they rock almonds in a pan filled with sugar and hot syrup, a candy shell forms on the nuts

Penny Candy

Can you remember the first time you held coins in your hand and were let loose in a candy store? Perhaps you lingered over your selection, then, once it was paid for, hid it in a special spot, looked at it off and on, and finally took a bite? Or did you know exactly what you wanted? Did you buy it, jam five in your mouth, and gulp them down as fast as possible?

In the late 1800s, children became candy consumers. Sweets were made, displayed, priced, and targeted at kids. You chose such treats as malted-milk balls, licorice strings, wax bottles filled with sweet liquid, or hard pellets of candy dots stuck on strips of paper. Like now, candy was available at the local general store, where tantalizing jars of bulk sweets lined the counter. You pointed to your choices and the sweets were scooped out, weighed, and bagged by the shopkeeper.

Hundreds of new candies were created each year, but only a few passed the test of picky young shoppers. Candy-makers tried every angle, claiming sweets

c. A.D. 1650   A.D. 1655   A.D. 1656   A.D. 1669

● ENGLAND: people develop a sweet tooth for black licorice candy coins

● JAMAICA: rum is made from distilled sugarcane and replaces beer as the drink of British sailors

● ENGLAND: Oliver Cromwell and Colonial Pride start a table fight throwing wet suckets

● UNITED STATES: Dutch settlers make and sell the first chocolate candies in North America

were good for you, cured sore throats, headaches, and the blahs. During the depression in the 1930s, candy with dextrose was approved by the American Medical Association. If kids didn't care, parents probably did.

Fifty years ago, when a few pennies paid for lots of sweets, kids knew where to invest for the greatest return. At three for a penny, black balls – hard, mild licorice-flavored candies that turn tongues purplish black and change color as they melt in your mouth – were a popular choice. Not for the squeamish, it was common practice to take out the black ball and show off the current color before popping it back in.

All-day suckers were the lollipop equivalent of a candy marathon. They lasted so long that the taste buds on your tongue stood up and shrieked with pain from the friction of slurping for hours. Pixy Stix, strawberry marshmallows, fizzy sherbets, jellies, jujubes, gum balls: your penny-candy list went on.

Today, kids go crazy for candies that fizz, explode, suck the saliva out of your mouth, or are so hot your eyebrows sweat. Candies no longer cost pennies, but bulk stores usually have a nostalgia section, where sweets such as black balls can still be found. How long can you make one last?

A.D. 1674

● ENGLAND: Thomas Willis, physician to the king, connects the body's use of sugar to diabetes

Home Sweet Home

When Granny and Janie make vanilla fudge, they work as a team. With a smile or a frown, they tell each other whether this will be a good batch; when they'll take their first bite.

The brown-sugar canister clunks down on the counter. Beside it go the bottles of corn syrup and vanilla extract. Out of the fridge come the butter and milk. Janie digs inside the pot cupboard and hauls out the heavy old pot with its sturdy handle. They tie aprons around each other's waists. Granny takes her candy thermometer out of its special sleeve and rests it well back on the counter. Getting the temperature right is the key to good fudge. Janie finds the wooden spatula, measuring cup, and spoons. Then they lay pot holders at the ready as well as a greased cake tin. They double-check their supplies and both nod with satisfaction. Oh, but they forgot the bowl of ice water. Now they're ready to start.

Janie measures 2 cups of brown sugar, 2 tablespoons of corn syrup, 1/2 cup of milk, and 1 1/2 tablespoons of butter into the pot. Granny lifts the pot onto the stove, turns the burner on medium, and stirs the ingredients until the sugar dissolves. The mixture bubbles and sweet smells tease Janie's nose. Granny can tell when

A.D. 1709

GERMANY: Gabriel Fahrenheit introduces his alcohol thermometer, used by doctors before confectioners. In 1714, he constructs the first mercury-in-glass thermometer.

A.D. 1713

SPAIN: the British South Sea Company is allowed to sell 4,800 African slaves per year to Spanish plantation owners

A.D. 1721

JAPAN: the Shogun bans luxuries, including candy, to save money

the fudge is almost ready, but it seems to take forever. She slides her thermometer into the pot. Janie watches the red liquid shoot up the scale and hover at 120°C (248°F). Granny puts on oven mitts, pulls the thermometer out, and lets a few drops of hot liquid fudge drop into the ice water. Janie dips her fingers in and rolls it into a firm ball. *Yup!* It's cooked.

Granny removes the pot from the heat and they let it cool for about five minutes. Then Janie adds a teaspoon of vanilla extract, licks the spoon, and gets a full rush of flavor in her mouth. She takes first turn beating the batter and when it gets too stiff for her, passes the spatula to Granny, who continues beating until the fudge is nearly set. Then Granny places the still-warm candy in the cake tin. She spreads it evenly into the corners and Janie runs a kitchen knife over the top, making it smooth. A few minutes later, they mark the top of the fudge with lines, where they'll cut it when it's cool. Like most candy-makers, Granny and Janie keep their recipe within the family, but they share it with you now.

A.D. 1732

FRANCE: Monsieur Dubuisson invents a table mill for grinding chocolate

A.D. 1747

GERMANY: Andreas Marggraf discovers that beets and carrots are a source of sucrose

CHOCOLATE

The World's First Chocoholics

Near the earth's equator, where temperatures are hot, air is humid, and it rains regularly, the cacao tree grows. Small and delicate, it needs overhead shade when young and thrives, with good soil, under rubber and banana trees. Unlike most plants, it blooms and fruits all year long.

An Olmec Discovery

Historians think that sometime between 1500 and 400 B.C., an Olmec living in Veracruz or Tabasco, Mexico, looked at this native evergreen and plucked a plump, melon-shaped pod from its trunk. She cracked it open, revealing a milky, gooey pulp surrounding about thirty beans. With cocoa beans from the cacao tree, chocolate had been discovered!

A Mayan Product

Neighboring Mayans learned how to process chocolate from the Olmecs. Beans were sun-dried, roasted, their shells removed. Then the nibs were ground on a stone, heated over a fire, patted into cakes, and left to cool and harden on banana leaves.

A.D. 1763

A.D. 1769

A.D. 1773

● FRANCE: Louis XV gives Canada to the English, but keeps the sugar-rich islands of Martinique and Guadeloupe

● UNITED STATES: oil is extracted from peanuts and hogs pig out on the leftovers

● ITALY: Pope Clement XIV dies – possibly from poison in his chocolate drink

Cocoa drinks were made from broken-up cakes. Mayan royalty and the elite drank chocolate as a bitter, frothy drink. They poured cocoa powder and water from one cup to another and created foam. Mayan soldiers added red dye to the powder, turning the surface of the drink blood red, and drank it as a pre-battle ritual. Important Mayans were buried with the tools to make a chocolate drink, including beautiful porcelain pots to hold cocoa powder.

An Aztec Addiction

The Aztecs acquired cocoa by trade, and merchants grew wealthy importing and selling the new luxury item. Aztecs liked their "chocolatl" frothed too, but added vanilla, honey, or chili peppers for flavor. In the early 1400s, King Tezozomoc offered visitors cocoa from drinking goblets made from polished tortoiseshell trimmed with gold. During his reign, from 1502 to 1520, Emperor Montezuma II was a chocoholic, drinking fifty cups of chocolatl a day. Montezuma liked drinking his chocolate cold and sent runners to the mountains for snow. Did Montezuma invent the North American snow cone?

A Spanish Secret

Montezuma II served chocolate to visitors, including the Spanish explorer Hernan Cortés in 1519. After toasting one another, Cortés returned the hospitality by taking over Montezuma's territory, including the cacao plantations. Cortés took cocoa beans and recipes back home and launched a love affair between the Spanish and chocolate. For years, the Spanish planted cacao trees throughout their New World colonies, while keeping chocolate secret from the rest of Europe.

How did the world remain in the chocolate dark for so long and who let chocolate out?

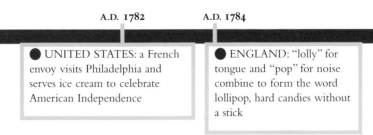

A.D. 1782

A.D. 1784

● UNITED STATES: a French envoy visits Philadelphia and serves ice cream to celebrate American Independence

● ENGLAND: "lolly" for tongue and "pop" for noise combine to form the word lollipop, hard candies without a stick

Chocolate Goes Global

"**A**rgh, matey! T'were dangerous times, sailing the high seas with the likes of Cortés. But I'd give up me wooden leg to have back the booty we burnt!"

In 1579, English pirates captured a ship bound for Spain. Leaping into the hold, they examined their prize – funny-smelling, dried-out, brown, what? They set the ship afire, disgusted that anyone would take a load of sheep poop across the ocean. In their ignorance, they had torched a small fortune in cocoa beans.

Feeding Spain's chocolate addiction brought a steady stream of cocoa beans from their New World colonies. The dark side of this secret was that slave labor produced the cocoa. And Spaniards preferred their chocolate sweet, which required the importation of sugar, also grown on slave plantations.

Wealthy Spanish women gathered in chocolate shops and even drank their frothy beverage in church. They convinced their priests that chocolate prevented fainting spells and was a healthy food substitute during times of religious fasting. It could have been priests who "spilled the beans" by confessing their fondness for chocolate while traveling outside of Spain. Or, Anne, daughter of Phillip II of Spain, could have told her husband, King Louis XIII of France. However, once the secret was out, there was no going back, and chocolate became an instant European status symbol.

France and England followed Spain's lead – importing chocolate and selling it to the elite. By 1615, chocolate was fashionable in the French royal court and was used to sweeten women's marriage dowries. In 1657, chocolate beverage houses opened in England, where cocoa was served to men only. It's been

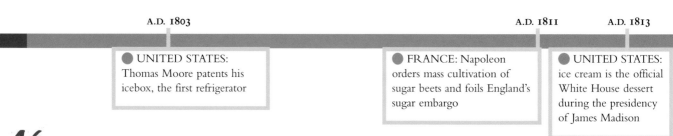

A.D. 1803

● UNITED STATES: Thomas Moore patents his icebox, the first refrigerator

A.D. 1811

● FRANCE: Napoleon orders mass cultivation of sugar beets and foils England's sugar embargo

A.D. 1813

● UNITED STATES: ice cream is the official White House dessert during the presidency of James Madison

reported that King Charles II took advantage of the chocolate fad by charging a seventy-pence tax on each pound of cocoa beans.

The European appetite for chocolate was so intense that Spain lost the monopoly on growing cacao trees. The Dutch, French, and English started plantations in their own tropical colonies. All agreed with Carolus Linnaeus' opinion of chocolate. He was the botanist who gave the cacao tree its scientific name – *Theobroma cacao* – "food of the gods."

A.D. 1817

ENGLAND: the first written recipe for butterscotch taffy originates in Yorkshire, not Scotland as commonly thought

A.D. 1825

FRANCE: Brillat-Savarin, French food writer, records that chocolate makes people healthy and happy

Bean to Bar

In nature, there are amazing transformations. Caterpillars change to butterflies, and tiny babies grow into awesome soccer players, math whizzes, or even ballet dancers. But the cocoa bean doesn't become anything spectacular until processed by people.

Harvesting cocoa hasn't significantly changed since Olmec times. It's still done by hand and is labor-intensive. Harvesters snip ripe fruit from the cacao trees using long-handled tools with shears on one end. Other workers take basketsful to areas where the pods are opened by a few sharp whacks from a machete. The beans are scooped out and the remains are composted. The precious beans are put into crates or heaped into piles, where they heat up in the sun and ferment for up to a week, depending on the weather.

During fermentation, a chemical reaction takes place inside the beans, breaking down the sugar. The beans become less bitter and develop a rich chocolate flavor and color. The beans are then dried, either in sunlight or by electric heaters. Drying prevents rotting and makes the beans lighter for transporting to market.

When a shipment of beans arrives at a chocolate factory, a cleaning machine removes any unwanted debris. Then

A.D. 1827

ENGLAND: chemist John Walker uses gum arabic, sugar, and potash on the tip of "Lucifer," a match that ignites when struck on a rough surface

A.D. 1829

SWITZERLAND: after selling blocks of chocolate for ten years, François Louis Cailler claims to make the first "candy bar"

the beans are roasted at 121°C (250°F) in a big rotating cylinder until they turn a deep brown. After cooling, the outer shell of the bean is cracked and blown off, leaving the valuable "nib." The nibs are crushed, or milled between stones or steel discs. The mill's rubbing action creates heat that turns the oil in the bean to a liquid called cocoa butter. The remaining solids are cooled, crushed, and sieved into fine cocoa powder.

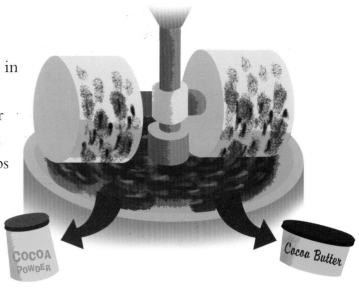

All pure chocolate candy starts with cocoa powder and cocoa butter. Different tastes are achieved by varying the quantities of cocoa butter and powder and by adding other ingredients, such as nuts, vanilla, milk, butter, or caramel. Over the years, chocolate-makers have tinkered with additives, improving and inventing new chocolate products.

Several companies claim to have created the first chocolate bar, including the Canadian company Ganong Bros. Limited. George Ensor, Ganong's talented candy-maker, created a chocolate-and-nut snack for family picnics and fishing trips. It was so popular with kids that Ganong produced a five-cent chocolate bar for sale in 1898, two years ahead of Hershey's famed bar. At that price, some kids could finally buy chocolate.

A.D. 1840

A.D. 1846 A.D. 1847

● UNITED STATES: the first dental college in the world opens in Baltimore, Maryland

● UNITED STATES: Nancy Johnson designs and makes the first hand-cranked ice-cream maker

● ENGLAND: Tom Smith tucks sugarcoated almonds and love notes inside colored tissues, making the first Christmas crackers

Chocolate's Good Chemistry

He's sat beside you all term – quiet, cute, and shy. But, on a mid-February morning, he opens his backpack and pulls out a small, heart-shaped box. He smiles, revealing red elastics on his braces. Slowly he reaches across the aisle and drops a Valentine token onto your desk. It's your favorite kind of chocolate. *How did he know? Could this be love?*

Let's try that again. . . . He reaches across the aisle and drops a shiny plastic bag of candies onto your desk. Inside you find Irish potato, molasses, chow mein, and vinegar candies. *What was he thinking?*

There is something about the chemistry of chocolate that goes right to the heart. Precisely 380 chemicals combine to work their magic on people. Scientists have discovered that with chocolate in your system, you feel happy.

Chocolate makes your brain produce opioid – a natural drug – that soothes your mood and acts like a painkiller. Another chemical in chocolate speeds up your pulse, making you feel perky. And cocoa butter softens at human body temperature, melting on your lips like a velvety kiss.

Eating chocolate mimics the sensations people feel when they fall in love. The average American must "feel the love" a lot – they eat 5 kg (11 lb.) of chocolate a year. That's probably more than parsnips, brussels sprouts, and rutabagas combined. Milk chocolate is candy – a sweet treat with little nutritional

A.D. 1850

● ENGLAND: doctors discover adding metals to color boiled candies is dangerous and the practice ends
● UNITED STATES: jawbreakers are popular hard candies

A.D. 1853

● UNITED STATES: Chef George Crum invents potato chips at the Moon Lake Lodge resort in Saratoga Springs, New York

value. But scientists classify dark chocolate as a beneficial food. One Harvard University study shows that people who eat dark chocolate live longer because it appears to reduce the risk of heart attack, stroke, and diabetes.

Science has given chocolate lovers another excuse to eat their favorite treat. Dark chocolate has been found to be a rich source of flavonoids – antioxidants that help the blood. Blueberries, apples, and onions have flavonoids, but nothing beats dark chocolate in the flavonoid department. So why don't we have a diet of dark chocolate? Because fruits and veggies have other nutrients the body needs and less fat than chocolate.

So, when you eat Halloween kisses, a solid Easter bunny, or Valentine chocolates, consider the chemistry. If it's dark chocolate, it's got more than flavor – it's got flavonoids and it could even cause your sweetheart to fall in love with you.

● RUSSIA: Elena Molokhovets' book, *Classic Russian Cooking: A Gift to Young Housewives*, suggests making gummy confections from wild strawberries, mint, or mushrooms
● ENGLAND: Richard Cadbury packages his Valentine's Day chocolates in a heart-shaped box

Chocolate Perfection

"Too many cooks spoil the broth," Great-Auntie used to say, but it was the combined efforts of many keen chocolate "cooks" that produced the variety of candies available today. Some contributed mechanical inventions; others improved cooking techniques; but it was all in search of the perfect chocolate treat.

If you take cocoa powder out of the cupboard and try mixing it into a glass of milk, what happens? Your big spoonful of powder just sits on the surface and doesn't blend well with the milk, no matter how much you stir. In the early 1800s, a Dutchman named Conrad J. van Houten was frustrated by the same problem and found that if he combined alkaline salts with cocoa powder, the mixture dissolved well in water. This process became known as "dutching." In 1828, van Houten made another contribution when he invented the cocoa press. This device squeezed more cocoa butter out of every bean and also made chocolate smoother.

Henri Nestlé, a Swiss pharmacy assistant, dabbled in a laboratory and developed the first powdered milk formula. As a byproduct of his experiments, he perfected condensed milk – a key ingredient in

A.D. 1875

UNITED STATES:
George Green patents the electric dental drill

milk chocolate. In 1875, his friend Daniel Peter mastered the process of combining milk and cocoa powder, which paved the way for mass-producing chocolate milk and milk chocolates.

In 1879, Rodolphe Lindt, of Swiss chocolate fame, invented a machine that made chocolate melt in your mouth. His "conching" machine rolled and heated the chocolate until it was buttery smooth. He then added more cocoa butter to the conched chocolate, creating a mixture known as fondant. This creamy form of chocolate is used as the basis for icings and in the centers of individual chocolates and chocolate bars.

Ruth Wakefield took chocolate to a whole new level when she invented chocolate chip cookies in 1924. She ran out of melting chocolate and, like any good cook, found a substitute. She chopped up a Nestlé's chocolate bar and discovered that the baked cookie had bits of solid chocolate inside. The cookies were a real hit and eventually she sold her recipe to Nestlé in return for a lifetime supply of chocolate. It's impossible to calculate the number of chocolate chip cookies made after that first batch, but like many sweet recipes, it started with a lucky substitution.

A.D. 1886

A.D. 1888

A.D. 1893

A.D. 1896

● UNITED STATES: John Pemberton, a pharmacist in Georgia, makes the first bottled Coca-Cola and sells it as a cure for headaches

● UNITED STATES: Thomas Adams designs a vending machine and sells Tutti-Frutti gum in New York City train stations

● CANADA: William Neilson sells his first block of ice cream in Toronto

● AUSTRIA: Leo Hirshfield and his daughter, nicknamed Tootsie, immigrate to the United States with their recipe for Tootsie Rolls

Daniel of Vancouver

Daniel believes chocolate is a food group. Growing up in Belgium, he let chocolate sit in his mouth until it melted. He savored each morsel, so he'd be the last one in the family to swallow his chocolate treat. This patience and control infuriated his sister. Sometimes she teased or tricked Daniel's last piece away from him, but she never robbed him of his passion for it.

When Daniel and his wife visited British Columbia in 1979, they loved everything about the place, except there was no Belgian chocolate. When they moved to Vancouver in 1981, they opened a shop in the hub of the city. Here they made chocolates in the back, sold them in the front, and locked the door when they sold out. Opening day at the end of July was a near disaster. Temperatures soared over 30°C (86°F) and, without air conditioning, the chocolates were melting as fast as they could sell them. During their first December rush, Daniel worked twenty hours a day. Too tired to drive home, he caught a few hours' sleep in his car. Daniel served coffee and chocolate to his customers in the lineup down Robson Street, and when he sold the last piece around two o'clock, he started making more for the next day.

Scrupulous and persnickety, Daniel is a chocolate purist. He uses only the best of natural, organic ingredients and so his chocolates are a little expensive. Daniel never cuts corners – when a bolt fell off a screw on the production line and ended up in a chocolate, he immediately installed a magnetic screening system. Now every chocolate is scanned before going into its box. And he allows no preservatives. If hydrogenated fat was added, his chocolates would last two years, but to Daniel, that would be cheating and unhealthy. His chocolates stay fresh for four weeks. If they sit on a shelf any longer, they begin

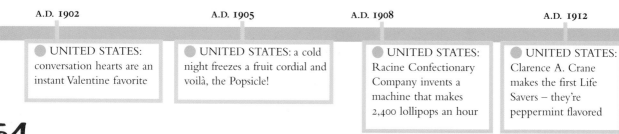

A.D. 1902

● UNITED STATES: conversation hearts are an instant Valentine favorite

A.D. 1905

● UNITED STATES: a cold night freezes a fruit cordial and voilà, the Popsicle!

A.D. 1908

● UNITED STATES: Racine Confectionary Company invents a machine that makes 2,400 lollipops an hour

A.D. 1912

● UNITED STATES: Clarence A. Crane makes the first Life Savers – they're peppermint flavored

to "bloom" – fat pops to the surface and creates a gray dust on the chocolate. But it's hard to imagine a Daniel chocolate in bloom.

If you ever buy one, put it on your tongue and let it melt. Daniel does this every working day. And, at the age of fifty-six, he still has amazing control. He eats only one.

A.D. 1922

GERMANY: Hans Riegel introduces dancing bears, later called Gummi Bears

A Sweet Story of Success

For those who know chocolate, the name Hershey means success. But for Milton Snavely Hershey, money did not always grow on cacao trees. Born in 1857 to humble Pennsylvanian farming folk, he left school after grade four and became a printer's apprentice. He soon switched trades and worked for a confectioner. At eighteen, with family help, he started his own candy business in Philadelphia, but after six years he returned home broke. For a year he roamed the country, learning the art of caramel-making in Denver and working in Chicago and New York. Hershey then started the Lancaster Caramel Company in 1886, selling the wildly successful Crystal A Caramels.

For ten years Hershey devoted himself to caramels, until he discovered chocolate at the 1893 World's Colombian Exposition in Chicago. He was so impressed with a display of German chocolate-making equipment that he bought it and took it home. At first, Hershey began by selling chocolate-coated caramels; later he added cocoa powder, baking and sweet chocolate to his product list. In 1900, he sold his caramel company for one million dollars because to him, "Caramels are only a fad. Chocolate is a permanent thing."

Milton Hershey never looked back. He bought a huge piece of land in Pennsylvania dairy country and built what remains the largest chocolate and cocoa factory in the world. With a steady supply of milk from the neighboring farms, he concentrated on producing milk chocolate, including the original Hershey Milk Chocolate bar. As his company grew, Hershey built a community for his workers, with housing, transit, recreational facilities, and schools. In 1906, the town was renamed Hershey. Now it's known as "The Sweetest Place On Earth," complete with streetlights in the shape of Hershey's Kisses.

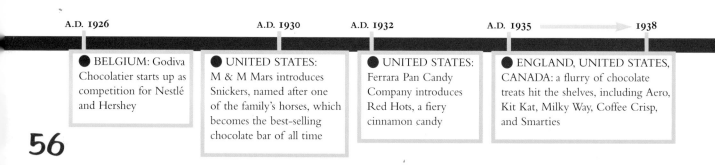

A.D. 1926

A.D. 1930

A.D. 1932

A.D. 1935   → 1938

● BELGIUM: Godiva Chocolatier starts up as competition for Nestlé and Hershey

● UNITED STATES: M & M Mars introduces Snickers, named after one of the family's horses, which becomes the best-selling chocolate bar of all time

● UNITED STATES: Ferrara Pan Candy Company introduces Red Hots, a fiery cinnamon candy

● ENGLAND, UNITED STATES, CANADA: a flurry of chocolate treats hit the shelves, including Aero, Kit Kat, Milky Way, Coffee Crisp, and Smarties

Hershey's legacy is more than sweet. Without children of their own, Milton and his wife, Catherine, started a school for orphaned boys in 1909. When Catherine died in 1918, Hershey entrusted his stocks to this school, now called the Milton S. Hershey School. Over a thousand children from underprivileged families still attend each year. And the money that pays for it comes from beans on cacao trees.

A.D. 1947

● CANADA: kids on Vancouver Island protest outside confectionary shops when the five-cent bar jumps to eight cents

CANDY MAGIC

Eye Candy

This is how it works. The big three companies – Nestlé, Mars, and Hershey – want to be at the front of the line and push and shove for that position. They pay huge fees to popular stores for the best "slot." So, when you look at a rack of candy and your eyes fall on its bar first, the candy companies are getting their money's worth and sometimes *your* money.

And they have other tricks up their sleeve to catch your eye. . . .

The expression "If it ain't broke, don't fix it" applies to candy wrappers. As soon as a product starts to sell, the package stays the same – even for a century. Buying candy can be a quick grab – "There's my favorite, I'll get that." If the package or design changes, you have to hunt for what you want and another brand might catch your eye. Sales research shows that people recognize the color of a package first, then the shape of the logo, and finally, the name of the product.

A candy by any name would still taste sweet, so why choose names that include body parts, such as Mozart's Eyeballs or Bonaparte's Ribs? Just for fun! How about candies with quirky names, such as Oh Henry! and Milk Duds? The names don't tell you much about the product, but they do grab your attention. A flirty shop girl used to shriek "Oh Henry!" when her boyfriend visited her at work. Would "Oh Howard!" have been a top-selling chocolate bar? Who knows! Milk Duds were supposed to be perfectly round, but a

A.D. 1954

A.D. 1962   A.D. 1963   A.D. 1964

● UNITED STATES: Just Born, Inc. introduces Marshmallow Peeps for Easter – now 4.2 million are made every day

● UNITED STATES: kids go crazy for sour candies, such as Lemonheads and SweeTarts

● CANADA: Hershey opens a factory in Smiths Falls, Ontario, but no Hershey kiss streetlights here

● UNITED STATES: British novelist Roald Dahl publishes *Charlie and the Chocolate Factory*

mechanical problem made them all different shapes. Nearly tossed out as "duds," they were rescued from the candy scrap heap because they tasted terrific.

If a zippy name won't attract customers, companies try gimmicks.

Otto Schnering, president of the Curtiss Candy Company, scored a big hit in 1923 when he dropped thousands of Baby Ruth bars from a plane over Pittsburgh. However, he did not score with baseball hero Babe Ruth, who was annoyed the name was so close to his own.

Depression candy had names such as Chicken Dinner, Original Boston Baked Beans, Tummy Full, and Vegetable Sandwich, suggesting you'd bought a real meal.

PEZ started out as a breath mint for smokers, but caught on as a candy with a collectable toy for kids. Recently one PEZ dispenser sold for a record $4,500.00. Now, that's eye-popping candy.

A.D. 1972

ENGLAND: John Yudkin, professor of nutrition in London, publishes the book *Pure, White and Deadly*, condemning white sugar

Mother's Sweet and Nut Shop

The bell at the top of the door jingles as you step into Mother's Sweet and Nut Shop. You pat the packages of sour-berry jellies, marshmallow hotdogs, and blue candy floss while waiting for Lina. She's busy slicing off a piece of fudge for Mr. Smith, who visits every day at the same time and buys the same thing. Lina wraps the fudge, smiles, and says, "Sixty-five cents, please." Then she turns and you ask, "What's new?"

"Well . . . ," Lina says, and takes you on a wonderful tour, past all the strange and familiar candies to the latest picks. You must choose between Snot – juicy candy that's dispensed through the nostrils of a plastic human nose; new jelly-bean flavors – earwax, vomit, dirt, and spaghetti (and they really taste like them, says Lina); an authentic Wonka Bar; and *Fear Factor*'s slimy gummy octopus, swimming in a bath of sour ooze. *Yuck – yum – ack!* How to decide?

Twenty-three years ago, Lina opened her candy store. She'd just retired from teaching school and knew how to get along with her customers. And she'd be living a dream from her childhood by surrounding herself with chocolate. It didn't take much to persuade her sister Susie to become her business partner. Today, Lina samples the new candies (even the weird ones), goes to sweet shows, and is a stickler for taste and quality. She asks herself, "Would I buy this for my child?" She also knows that kids want trendy and crazy treats that they'll buy once, on a dare or just for fun. Susie is not often tempted. After all these years, she's had her fill of candy. But sometimes, when it's busy, she has choco-late for supper.

Together, Lina and Susie have watched hundreds of children grow up. They know that if you're a little kid, you'll love lollipops. As a five-to-seven-year-old, you'll go for a cool colorful package with a gimmick or gadget as well as the

A.D. 1975	A.D. 1978	A.D. 1982
UNITED STATES: B.F. Feingold links artificial flavor and color to hyperactivity	UNITED STATES: Dan White uses the "Twinkie defense" at his murder trial, saying too much sugar made him do it	UNITED STATES: Reese's Pieces become a craze with the movie *E.T.*

sweet. If it's supersour, blazing hot, or sticks to everything, at seven to nine you'll buy it. You like grossing out your parents and outlasting your friends, even if your tongue is on fire. By ten, you're more sensible about candy choices and want good value and taste. As a teenager, you zero in on favorite brands that you'll love forever. Lina and Susie watch closely in order to satisfy all customers – toddlers, tweens, and teens. And they may not know every name, but they never forget a face.

A.D. 1988

● CANADA: Ganong breaks into the Japanese candy market, exporting container ships full of Delecto chocolates

A.D. 1996

● SOUTH AFRICA: the KwaZulu-Natal Rotary Club makes a chocolate and marshmallow Easter egg, over 7.6 m (25 ft.) long and weighing 4,068 kg (8,968 lb.)

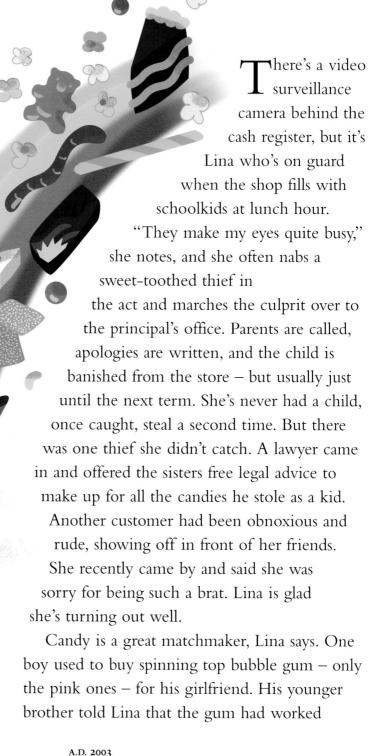

There's a video surveillance camera behind the cash register, but it's Lina who's on guard when the shop fills with schoolkids at lunch hour. "They make my eyes quite busy," she notes, and she often nabs a sweet-toothed thief in the act and marches the culprit over to the principal's office. Parents are called, apologies are written, and the child is banished from the store – but usually just until the next term. She's never had a child, once caught, steal a second time. But there was one thief she didn't catch. A lawyer came in and offered the sisters free legal advice to make up for all the candies he stole as a kid. Another customer had been obnoxious and rude, showing off in front of her friends. She recently came by and said she was sorry for being such a brat. Lina is glad she's turning out well.

Candy is a great matchmaker, Lina says. One boy used to buy spinning top bubble gum – only the pink ones – for his girlfriend. His younger brother told Lina that the gum had worked

A.D. 2002

● UNITED STATES: Tootsie Rolls celebrate their 100th anniversary on the New York Stock Exchange

A.D. 2003

● UNITED STATES: the largest s'more ever weighs 725.7 kg (1,600 lb.), using 20,000 marshmallows, 7,000 chocolate bars, and 24,000 graham crackers

because his brother was now going steady. Then he picked out a bag of pink spinning tops. She hopes it'll work its magic on his sweetheart, too.

Have you made up your mind yet? Take a clear plastic bag and walk around the small, stuffed shop once more. Some sour strips will keep your eyes open while you study French verbs. A box of retro gobstoppers will make Dad happy, and Mom likes the nasty purple gum that tastes like soap. Perhaps you'll get your sister the candy that cracks and explodes in your mouth, even though she's not likely to share. And finally, some Jelly Bellies. Earwax, dirt, and spaghetti. Not the vomit. That's just too awful. But maybe a couple to slip into your uncle's hand – just to see what happens. Okay, and two pink spinning tops because it's nearly Valentine's. And if you chicken out, you can always chew them yourself.

The bell at the top of the door clangs again as you walk out, swinging your bag of loot. Lina and Susie wave and get busy with other customers. They really are two kids in a candy shop who like it when their customers live happily ever after.

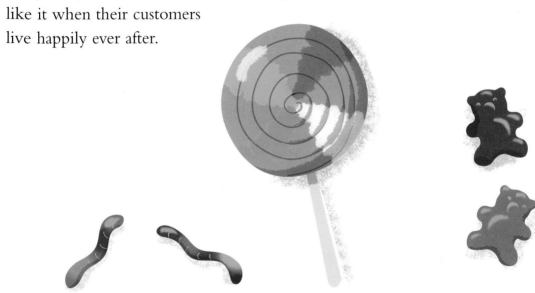

A.D. 2005

● CANADA: grade-six math students from Thunder Bay, Ontario, calculate that the 4 billion Smarties Canadians eat every year would circle the world once

A.D. 2006

● UNITED STATES: Jelly Belly Candy Co. makes about 120 million Jelly Belly jelly beans a day
● CYBERSPACE: a Google search lists more than 110,000 hits for candied insects, including chocolate ants, brittle scorpions, and root-beer-flavored cricket suckers

Authors' Note

or How We Wrote a History of Humankind from the Point of View of Candy . . .

From ancient times through the Middle Ages, "sweet" discoveries and inventions were not well documented. Sometimes people deliberately kept information about sweets secret. In 500 B.C., the Persians tried to keep sugarcane a secret and, two thousand years later, the Spanish did the same with chocolate. Even today, big candy factories sometimes blindfold repair workers. Because so much money and fame are made from candy, a number of people may claim to be the sole inventor and the courts have to decide on the patent. And, over the years, candy-makers have spun legends to add mystery and interest to marketing their product. Getting at the truth has been fun, fascinating, and sometimes frustrating.

Determining accurate dates is often difficult. For ancient times, reliable sources can refer to an era, a dynasty, or a lifetime, e.g., "during the Roman Empire." This makes sense – it takes time for a small discovery or invention to catch on and be recorded. Where we couldn't pinpoint an exact date, we selected one midtime frame and used the symbol *c* for "circa" to indicate our date is approximate. Where we could be a little more precise, we offered a date, again using the symbol *c*. In more modern times, where sources differed or contradicted each other, we selected dates supported by at least two reliable sources.

In the time line, we used modern place names, such as Iran and Italy, followed by historical names for peoples, such as the Persians and the Venetians.

In the case of some sweets, such as lollipops and ice-cream cones, there are many claims to invention. And for some candies, the actual dates of invention, patent, first production, and first sale were years apart. Once again, we included claims and selected dates that were supported by two reliable references.

We weren't able to verify how runny caramel gets inside a certain chocolate bar, but we have a good idea. And it's based on science, not legend!